Speak

poems by Jay Rossier

with a preface by Kelley McKenna Rossier
and introduction by John Reinhart

Cover design by Patrick Reinhart

Photo of the boy by Jason Rosewell;
photo of the the older man by Joshua Ness.

ISBN-13: 978-1978029392
ISBN-10: 197802939X

For Sam, Liam, Lily, Claire

and Kelley

Contents

Preface

My late husband, Jay Rossier, compiled this collection before he died in May 2012. Most of the poems were written during the last year of his life when he wrestled, not just physical illness, but with his understanding of what it means to be fully human in the face of death. Jay found the beautiful and the wretched equally fascinating and worthy of intellectual and emotional understanding. He approached poetry in this way as well. He would often meditate on one line of poetry by Heaney or Bishop or Auden, as if he was trying to embody the poets' words, yearning to know both the anguish and the sublime of each phrase. Deeper, he wanted to go, and deeper still. In the last year of his life, beyond the daily struggles of a body that was slowly deteriorating, his world revolved around his children, his relationship to something beyond this world and poetry.

The poems in this collection are filled with love and anger. Jay raged against his illness, against God and against those he felt he should have raged against long ago. In this way, he was released from the prison he'd come to know as a human being. He reared his head, roared loudly, and spoke the truth he needed to express. At the end of his life, because he was able to finally break free from the entrapment of depression, or rage turned inward, he was able to forgive the people and circumstances of his life. In this forgiveness, he came to know a freedom he'd never known before. And his death, although unbearably sad for those he left behind, was full of peace and light.

He titled the collection, *Speak*, because this is what he learned to do. His message was, and is, "Speak your anger, speak your pain, speak your love–expose the depth of your heart. Don't hold back."

Kelley McKenna Rossier
Aberystwyth, Wales

Introduction

> *"Love is the one thing we're capable of perceiving*
> *that transcends dimensions of time and space."*
> ~ Dr. Brand, from *Interstellar*

I wandered in to the registration table to pick up my packet of materials. First day of graduate school. Many of the students, far more than would be in our class, had already been there for a week. Teachers – so the university ran summer semesters. Teachers – so many of them, an overwhelming number, seemingly, were women. Middle aged-ish women too.

I just took my packet, already a little lost after an hour drive in the July heat. I found a quiet bench and sat. I opened the folder and began looking over the various schedules and information. The packet was a little less overwhelming than the exuberant women.

Someone sat down next to me. Another guy. I wasn't alone. "Anything good in there?" he asked.

This was Jay.

Over the next year, Jay went from a fellow traveler, to comrade, to friend. Driving his old Volvo station wagon, he carted several of us canoeing, or swimming in waterfalls, or just to socialize after classes on Friday afternoons.

Jay regaled us with stories of knitting while driving down the highway, raising pigs, and navigating life amid divorce, career change, and parenting two boys.

When graduate school was done, we went our separate ways – my soon-to-be wife and I headed back to my childhood home in Denver, Colorado, while Jay took a job teaching near his home in Vermont. Major life changes got in the way but never stopped us from keeping tabs on one another. We all stumbled through.

I remember some note or email that Jay was sick, surgeries, hospitals, then the cancer, more hospitals. It all seemed to happen so quickly.

> *Be well. Don't know if I'll make it to Colorado*
> *any time soon, but will be thinking of you*
> *until I see you all again somewhere.*

The last words Jay wrote to me, three months before his body gave out, still ring in my ears, and as I began writing more and more poetry,

3

Jay occasionally crept into the lines. I meet him there more often than I imagined I would, a little sad, but comforted by his presence.

In that last letter, Jay noted that he'd put together a poetry manuscript, examples of which he included as well. Five books into my own poetry career, still holding a copy of the four poems Jay sent me, I finally worked up the courage to get in touch with Kelley, Jay's wife, to ask about publishing the full manuscript. She graciously gave me permission to launch this book into space.

The poems here reflect several themes, returning several times to the characters of Job and Prospero, two sufferers, exiles, wrestling with what it means to live. In the whispering trees, in the experiences of his children, in relationship to animals, Jay's poetry circumscribes the picture of being human – which is usually a dirty, frustrating, difficult business, though beautiful too. In "Going Deeper," he writes

> I don't know all the concrete steps to take.
> I don't know what it is I'm supposed to do.
> I don't know what the tools are.
> I don't have the manual.

And yet by the end of "Fishing"

> And then,
> next day, nonplussed, not
> hopeful, tried again.

The new day dawns, Prospero is released, Job survives. There is a hopefulness in

Recycling Flotsam On The Beach In Maine

> The boys,
> with knives, turn floats –
> abandoned broken buoys
> all lost by fishermen upon the rocks –
> to boats.

Jay's poems weave and interweave, reflecting his familiarity with the poets who came before and his own sense of language, ultimately collaborating to find his voice. I am honored to help provide a venue for that voice, a voice I still hear in the shushing trees and the perfect pine by the chicken coop.

letting go

I heard you clearly
I keep reading your words
the only place left us to speak
of chicken scratchings
how is the weather?
again and again
you stood and took a moment
offering tears to water space

in my dreams
years later
willing you into this space
at the edge of my awareness
I reread your last letter
pierced by suffering
smiling between rounds
lost as you let go

John Reinhart
Denver, Colorado

Congenital

Every parent was a child:
we never will have outgrown this. By
children we remain beguiled, with
parents we remain remiss.

I Am Waiting, Too
(after Ferlinghetti)

I am waiting for that tooth to come in,
the molar on the bottom in the back
that keeps my one-year-old up, which
keeps the four-year-old up, which keeps
the rest of us up.
He's just gone down and at three-thirty
the windows are gray rectangles
in a black wall, and the wind
is starting out in the fence row.

The tooth is like the small sunflower
we planted in a pot in the living room in May.
Restless budding pushing up
through the gummy flesh
of an innocent who by day
grabs my legs, the chair, the wall, the cat,
and pulls himself up,
pleased with his successful grope
toward membership in the human race;
who vigorously points,
exhorting and explaining in words
of no other human's devising
why we should note the quaking leaf
of the aspen, the tiny ant on the kitchen floor.

Quarter to four. Still I am imagining
that I can hear his muffled restless cry,
while the wind shushes hopefully in the maples.

8

The Baltic Sea

The Baltic Sea lies
windless, horizon
another silver
strata of the still,
steel-colored overcast.
The air, too, is still.
The ships in the great
gray distance at first
infinitesimal,
dissolve. Follow them
into that smoky
oblivion, and,
eventually,
you'd get to Poland,
a place I've never
been and don't expect
I will ever go.

The sea keeps its own
counsel, the sea is
patient, knowing it
will know the moment
to open up its mouth
and let us all know
what is on its great
gray primeval mind.

Thanksgiving Day 2009

Three minutes to three. The sun just went down here,
in the living room, while she reads the paper
out loud, and I type. Three minutes to three,
about the time when other people are making the final preparations,
the creamed whole onions, the whipped mashed sweet potatoes,
the turkey probably out of the oven already
resting on the counter, the carving knife now just about to come out,
and we are here, the two of us, alone.
Don't get me wrong, there's nowhere I like better alone
than with her, no time, almost, when I wouldn't
rather be with her alone than wherever I am,
but here, now, it's two minutes past three,
both our kids gone with the exes,
and neither of us having made the plan
soon enough to have made any plan at all,
both of us grieving the loss
of the sun behind the trees,
of our kids to the exes, of our own separate youths,
when our mothers did the cooking,
and still lived with our fathers, and the table by this time of day
became crowded with cousins,
and there was somebody to watch the football game with
and there was a fire in the fireplace
and there was turkey and gravy. Today we didn't plan,
and so we'll eat what's left in the house: millet,
and broccoli sautéed with garlic.
We'll roast the chestnuts we found at the gas station.
Perhaps there are a few mustard greens left
in the garden after the latest frosts.
We have onions if we want to add those to the broccoli.
We put some beans on that should be done by the time
the first movie of our triple feature is over.
Perhaps later we'll go to the Joseph Smith Memorial, birthplace
of the Mormon leader, just ten minutes from here,
to watch their live nativity, and to see them flip the switch
on their 150,000 (so they advertise) Christmas lights.
And when the cow and donkey have been led in

and the swaddled baby, bawling, put in and out
of the manger, and the stars in the sky
obliterated by the 150,000 lights,
we'll come home, put on a fourth movie,
watch it till we fall asleep, and finally,
up in bed, under a deep pile of wool blankets,
kiss, so tenderly, as always, and hold on
to each other for the night.

Christmas Eve Eve

I stood peeing at the toilet the other day,
pushing as is now my post-surgery habit
to get the last of it out
and the feeling of whatever sphincter I'm opening up
became a picture-image in my head
of the slender bladder neck that now so famously
sports the little bit of positive margin
left behind, and I had a visitation,
not by an angel, but by a flash
of vivid understanding in both mind
and body, of my mortality: the margin,
ultimately, would grow, and gather me up
altogether like a mother
scooping up her tired little boy
after a long day, gathered first around the waist,
another hand on the bum, the torso
necessarily following, and then the limbs
tucked and folded in, like a bird,
settling on its perch for the night,
coddled and cooed over,
and finally sung to sleep.

Valentine With Chickens

The coop
retains its white
thick cap. The garden sleeps
under thick cover. All the gaunt
spare trees with naked arms beseech the air.
You are my quiet, whispering, perfect pine, still green.
Be mine.

Stoic

A boy begins his ninth year in the back
of an old station wagon, with a dog's head
in his lap, a burlap grain bag covering him up
where a truck has run over one of his hind legs.
The car is driving fast down the gravel road.
The dog lies still, in shock, until it rouses
and struggles with its eyes closed, working its jaws.
He thinks it's trying to bite him. Then it stops.
Stops moving, then stops breathing, and is still.

The car drove on. Did he say anything?
Try to whimper something to his mom?
Get them to stop? What was he thinking? What
cold overwhelm of fear and grief possessed him?
Or did he cry? Perhaps. But I think not.

Or was it as I now remember it:
the dog at death receding into two
dimensions, flattening out and drawing back
from him, receding like a road sign in
the rear view getting smaller, in his eyes
abstracting till the dog belonged
to someone else, to someone else's story
of that strange afternoon, the brakes, the dust,
the big rear tire bumping over something –
yelping flopping circles burlap wheel barrow,
and then him in the car, in the way back,
his legs cramped up, the dog's head on his lap?

Snapshots of a Life

I. Missing

When they did the first cat scan of my pelvis
they found I was missing a kidney.
Forty-eight years I'd been missing that kidney. More,
counting the time before I was born.
They said it had started to grow,
they don't know how much,
and then it just shriveled up,
they don't know exactly when.
There was a bit of the assembly left.
A piece of the ureter, by now grown fat
and sluggish. It had apparently
tried to plug in at the wrong spot.
Or something, in any case it didn't work,
the kidney disappeared
(I suppose they can see its ghost there somehow)
and the tube was left to fend for itself,
suspended in my pelvis
like a stillborn child. It lay there forty years
before the cancer arrived, coming
over the hill from the prostate,
ramifying the hell out of it.

II. Breakfast

I don't remember this either.
I've only been told the story:
I'm in my high chair,
a chrome and yellow one from the sixties.
Steel. It is very cold.
I am eating peas and spaghetti,
and when I have eaten all I want,
I turn the plate over
onto the floor. It wasn't empty. Someone,
my Mom I suppose, cleaned up the peas
and shards of the broken plate.
They haven't told me, perhaps they've forgotten
how many times it took
before they swapped out the fiesta ware
for a tin pie plate.
I don't know where I got the idea
that this was a trying time for my folks,
but I imagine my dad at this point in his life,
working like a fiend at the office all day,
coming home to his little kids
at that witching hour I learned to dread
sometime around suppertime, with his coat
over his arm, his briefcase
set down somewhere.
I don't know. I just imagine, given
the hot-tempered intolerant boom-voiced jerk that he was,
that the tossing of that plate on the floor
might have seemed to him a personal insult
or character flaw
that it was his personal responsibility
to correct
in me.

III. King of the Dads

One day, my eldest son at twelve years old
told me off. I don't remember about what.
I remember being pleased because at his age
I wouldn't dream of saying any such thing
to my old man, rusty man that he was.
So gloated I, King of the Dads, who reared a son
who wasn't afraid of me.
                              But now, at sixteen,
he tippy toes around me, trying so hard
to be careful that I can't figure out
what he wants to ask – I think
it's something that he thinks
will hurt me.

IV. Predisposition

Trailing clouds of glory do we come,
all of us. But trailing other shit, too.
The truth is, I don't know what happened in the kitchen that day
or any other day. What do I know
about flipping plates at six months old?
Seventeen thousand infants could have broken their dinner plates
(What parent feeds any kid on a breakable plate?
Perhaps one whose first child, my older sister, didn't make waves.)
without any problem. Another hundred and seventeen thousand
could have looked their exasperated (or worse) parent in the eye
and played dumb, pretending not to know
what they were so angry about.
Another one million one hundred thousand one hundred and seventeen
undoubtedly would decide the large human before them
was insane, and let it go.
Maybe chalk it up to one more grown-up hang up and be sympathetic,
for the moment that they thought about it, and go on
to dessert, that banana mashed up in the mueli grinder with oatmeal.
But I held onto it in my little clenched fists.
I held back, wanting (I wish) to spare the man
the full measure of my wrath. I was afraid
I'd blast him to pieces, and body parts
would scatter like at the scene
of a suicide bombing.
Too early, it has to be, for this to have been
learned behavior.

V. Tears

The summer I was eight years old, in August,
it was a good crabapple year, and ornamental trees
throughout the neighborhood were full,
with many on the ground. Kenny Lamb picked one up
and threw it at some other kid, who threw one back,
and so it started. In a few minutes, engulfed in the melee,
I caught one in the right eye, and ran home,
crying to my mother.
That was the last time I can remember crying
until Deirdre Enright dumped me
in my junior year in college. And even then
it was just a few choked sobs.
You could count them on one hand.
Where did all those tears go? Can you get through
elementary school, adolescence, freshman, sophomore year without so
much as one small muffled croak?
The water in my blood that would have been used
to make tears seeped into my stomach
and carried the caustic bitterness down, down.

Recycling Flotsam On The Beach In Maine

The boys,
with knives, turn floats –
abandoned broken buoys
all lost by fishermen upon the rocks –
to boats.

I

Parent, teacher, student, I:
A box of stones, a revelry,
Ten thousand starlets crying, "hush!"
A whispered eighth note, darkling thrush.
Amoeba swimming in a hole,
A bite of soup, a jelly roll,
An animal with teeth and claws,
A diamond hiding all its flaws.
Huck riding on the raft with Jim,
A scene played out behind a scrim,
A butler, baker, beadle, bore.
A splashing raindrop, nothing more.

Liam Among the Animals

No Saint Kevin this one,
sitting in a cell with his arms outstretched
waiting for the blackbirds to hatch, no,
he's running full tilt
across the yard after the chickens,
scattering gravel and feathers
in a maelstrom of flapping and squawking,
laughing at me when I yell at him to stop. Still,
he stops. And in spite of his sly smile
I half believe him when he says
he only wanted them to play.
                                              Yes,
it was your brother,
the farmer, three years older,
having bought in to the business
with several weeks' worth (a dozen hens)
of his nine-year-old's allowance,
who took some chicks to school for show and tell.
He was afraid to pick them up, so
he took you with him. And in the classroom watched
while with your gentle, ignorant confidence
you caught each bird up and held it in two hands
cupped like a nest, and with some innate admiration
for the naked beauty of a living thing, held it up
so each third grader could get a good look.

Day

If I could pray, if I
could just make myself stop
spinning in my head
long enough, a second,
an instant, time enough
to utter one thought-word
toward God, who hears all things,
said and unsaid, thought
and not-thought, it would be
a bloody fucking scream.

Easy

Despair
is easy, so
familiar, like the friend
whose thoughts you know though neither of
you speak.

Don't Let Me Ask It

Don't let me ask it:
what is there left to lose?
Because there is always more,
always more to be taken away,
to leave behind, as the case may be,
depending on your view of agency.
The cock crows. The light comes
and you wish you were dead,
no, it's only after, the aftertaste,
the lingering nightmare:
how long how long
lying beside her like a corpse
grateful not to be called to task
grateful not to hear her woes
grateful not to hear the reasons
she can't live like this any more
well, you can't live like this anymore either
take up your pallet and go home
take up your pallet and go home
take up your pallet and go home
take it up.

Invocation

The diagnosis now is last year's news.
The panic, the research, the interviews
of doctor after pompous, preening doctor;
surgery, and then recovery,
as least as far as anyone could *see*;
a bleak mid-winter of our discontent
on hormones, brief success, according to
the hocus pocus of the PSA,
and then recurrence.
                          Come to me then, Muse.
Come now, out from wherever it is you hide,
up in my brain, down in my gut – or did
you get resected with the dumb prostate?
Now that the spirits of the tiled floor
and cold disciples lying on their carts
are gathering outside to form their choir,
come whisper to me now, my easeful Death,
come sing me, soft and low, sweet lullabies,
and try to tell me something I don't know.

Leaving Humlegaarden Clinic

'Or do you,' the Lord asked for the last time, 'hold and believe
that I have resolved to create a sublime world, with all things
necessary to the purpose in it, and none left out?'
                    - Isak Dinesen, "The Cardinal's First Tale"

...and at once from your calm eyes,
With their lucid proof of apprehension and disorder, All we are
not stares back at what we are.
                    - W.H. Auden, "Prospero to Ariel"

O Prospero, Prospero,
alone on your island all
those years, did you prosper? Gulls
fight over clams on the beach.
Caliban lets loose a string
of clever obscenities.
Was it worth it? Did you get
what you wanted? Yes, I know
bountiful Fortune has now
washed ashore with Alonso
and the rest. Now, finally,
you can act on that inner
transformation that you seem
to have worked upon yourself.
I applaud you. What a long
slog it must have been, every day
the same breakfast banana,
coconut lunch, and God knows
what you might have conjured up
from monkey, say, or some large
flying insect for dinner.
What did you do with all that
time? Miranda's class could not
have been very demanding.
And Caliban, of course, was
a quick study, we know that.
Did you look after a pet?

A bird, perhaps a lizard?
Did you swim in the lagoon
after lunch? Or, now that you're
older, do you nap instead?
In the old days you must have
run hard with Ariel's tribe,
cooking up spells – to work on
whom? Turtles sunning themselves
on their swamp logs? Did you make
a show of fake smoke and fire
to ward off pesky real-life
mosquitoes? Did it keep you
amused, keeping Ariel
busy each morning, trying
out the tricks you taught yourself
the night before?

                   Prospero,
I am not old, not quite yet,
but somehow, since I was young,
Miranda's age, or Ferdinand's,
I played at being old, drank
Keats' Hippocrene in the woods,
by the Lake romanticized
disaster, imagined loss
till long past the time to get
down to business, figure out
who I needed to forgive,
and get on with it. Somehow
you stumbled on the courage
to lay aside all your books
and give up on illusion.
But how? How to tell after
so long whether what you saw
was the real thing or whether
you were merely sleepwalking?
Whether that soothing music
came out of your own sad head,
or instead from the real birds,

or from, without your input,
your instructions or your spells,
the nonsectarian and
entirely purposeless, un-
achieving Heavenly Spheres
themselves? How did you find out
that you were living within
a play within a play?
                                        You
regret moving on, I know.
Your list of achievements is
impressive, all that plucking
of pine and bedimming of
noontide sun. You are rightly
proud. Your time alone with your
twin recalcitrants – airy
Ariel and that other
Noisesome Slug – has served you well.

How is it that this lonely
place and its weird company
have helped you to navigate
to where you can distinguish
the thing that's truly living
from the pretty fantasy
that, let's face it, we all know
is dead.
            Like you, I am now
heading home, but not to die.
I've lived with you on my own
island here, and with a crew
of cancer-ridden inmates
long enough to figure out
that Death is not some sweet dream,
some fictional character
idly dropping by for tea,
bringing sweet jam and muffins
and the Great Deliverance.
I have sat down to breakfast

with a mother of young kids,
forty-two years old, tumors
in her pancreas doctors
say will do her in, and soon;
with a once-young grandfather,
unable to eat, laying
his head down on the table
instead, his color just like
silly putty, while his son's
son, having just learned to walk,
delighting in new freedom,
laughs and tugs at his pant leg.
If there's a mysterious
guest here its name is Courage.
These people know the tempest
they live in now is not a
tricked-up smoke and mirror show,
no cheap grandstanding of some
luckless has-been former Duke.
For though you have to look hard
and listen quite closely, fear
is here, too, quiet, endured.
What I aspire to now is this:
the humility that comes,
if we choose it, with old age
and which is available
as a bonus to those with
discernment and a chronic
disease. What I wish for now
is just to go home and be
with my boys and with Kelley.
And as I pull out of here –
leaving behind the Baltic
Sea, its moments of quiet
revelation, the hot box
where they cooked up a fever
to try to kill the cancer,
the pills and zaps, colored lights,
the Great Doctor Finn himself –

I'm taking your queer story
with me in the hope that by
your somewhat crude but wholly
human example, I might
drift, one day, into the world
as God made it, whole, alive.

Prospero to Jay

You do me honor, sir, with your quaint lines.
I am most humbled by your skill with words
and flattered by your kind attention, paid
to such an old and luckless has-been blow-
hard former ill-begotten sad-sack duke
as I. Your island, too, has taught you well,
and you are rightly thankful for't. But I
should like the chance to speak with you a time
and offer such advice as an old man,
bowed down with years and care, and parenting
alone a daughter now that's come of age,
and who like you has kept his nose in books,
sequestered in the study of his head –
sad head, I think you put it – might supply.

Humility – bah! Spare me the din of your chanting
humility, humility. Humility my ass! Get yourself
a cold beer and a TV football game on Sunday afternoon
if all you want is humility. You've crawled,
stubbled and stinking, like the prodigal himself
right up to the edge of the truth
and then stretched out for a nap in the sunshine
while God and His angels played pinochle
in the clouds at your feet, waiting around
for you to get your act together. Play
within a play? *A tale told by an idiot.*
What you aspire to is to wake up
and call bullshit on the fuckers of this world
wherever they are, in your family
in your household, in your head,
and let em have it right between the eyes.
Don't stint! And don't come back here
whining about grandstanding until
you've made a show of using your own throat.

Listen,
    you've gone to such great lengths to teach yourself

the ways and needs of everyone around;
to take such trouble observing everything
with such a painter's eye, or criminal's –
for purposes of celebrating daylight
or hiding from it isn't always clear;
to so assiduously study me,
for God's sake, an illusion of an illusion –
you flatter me. But let me just say this:
You know you're swimming in dangerous waters here,
with your forty-something mom gone terminal,
and grandpa's prancing toddler at his feet.
Those people don't need your prating
and disingenuous comparison.
But how, now that you've used them anyway,
could you arrive at such a dumb conclusion?

The lesson you should take home now from me,
if I may be so bold, is NOT to be like me,
all humbled and prepared to sail off now
for Naples and Milan and then "the earth."
You still, as you yourself say, are *not* old
and given your biography, the best
response to present circumstances, which,
okay, are not the best, is to let it fly:
don't shut up. Put away all that claptrap
and holier than thou do-gooder crap.

Humility is just what you don't need.
Gather your guts, don't chide yourself
for being in books, but please,
don't take from all your hard-won study
and fine reading of our master's works that you
should somehow be more kind, more thoughtful
than you have already been
year in, year out, since you were but a mewling,
puking thing in a high chair yourself.
Get on with it, as you yourself say,
vent your own frustrations like that
child you were before you got this big idea

that it was not okay to open your mouth
and speak.

Last August

They cut me open and scraped the cancer out.
It was all over the inside of my body. It had started down there, down
there in the abdomen, back behind where you have your
hard on and it flared out, infecting parts and organs
and tubes I never knew I had,
and another I was supposed to have but didn't.
One lymph node after another,
uncountable lymph node after lymph node, until the entire cavity up
under my rib cage had it and they don't know
where else it went after it ducked up
between my ribs, hidden in the twisting cords of my aorta
and whatever other tubes and conduits bring blood
and whatever else down and up and up and down,
from the heart to the loins and back, that conduit,
that line of communication, it started back there
and by the time it was all over
sex was dead.
Sex had been carved out with the prostate and put in the compost. Sex
was a casualty, sex was gone missing, sex was
eradicated altogether, they killed it
when they scalpeled out the cancer.

But I had written that story my own self years before,
complete with that unhappy ending,
in all my self glorifying self pity
and pretty melancholy, anger
brewing, caustic,
cold.

A Song
for Kelley

> *"Set me as a seal upon your heart as a seal upon your arm, for love is strong as death, passion fierce as the grave. Its flashes are flashes of fire, a raging flame."*
>
> — Song of Songs 8:6

Love of my life.
You have given me my freedom.
You have given me my life.

You woke me up to who I am.
I was afraid, and you saved me.
I was alone, and you came to me.

***

Love of my life, five Christmases now, and your eyes still shine.
When you walk in the door, my heart still leaps at your smile.
There is never a day, never a moment, when I am not happy to be with
 you.

In the early hours, you loved me, in the darkness you held my hand.
I was unable to trust, fear was my companion.
Grace now goes with me where only dread accompanied me.

I brought my old fears hidden, from childhood, from a bad marriage.
You accepted them, you didn't laugh at me, you didn't send me away.
You held me, you held them, you comfort me always.

To me you are never dull, you are never plain, you are never not
 beautiful.
In the morning with your head full of sleep, your golden hair tousled
you are beautiful to me.

In the morning when you first wake you are a gift, an angel
glowing white gold coming to me with your kisses,
with your kisses and sweet words.

36

In the evening, together in the dark, whispering about our days to each
    other
you hold my hand, you embrace me, you feed me with your words
and with the warmth of your body.

Your words are never dull to me, your stories never old,
your voice, my love, is always sweet to me. It restores me when I am
    weary.
I live in it, and love you in it.

Day after day you are a rare gift, offered by the universe, by God, for me
    – I love you.

* * *

Our love now has weathered the hardest difficulties,
sickness and ill health have come to our door
and because we are what our love has made us, we let him in.

We live with him now, we make the most of his stay with us.
He has not changed our love, but he has altered its face.
Sickness has had the power to change us, to transform us.

Your love of God has inspired me, has inspired mine.
Our trust in each other has given us strength,
strength to get through each day with joy and with gratitude.

I love you in the mornings, the sun streaming through our windows,
both of us working, writing together,
opening ourselves and each other, to ourselves and the world.

I love you in the evening, laughing together at our shows,
sitting beside you with my corn flakes,
children with us, or by ourselves.

I love you when it's hardest for both of us,
when I stand naked before you and you tend to my wounds;
when my family has poisoned you, has cut you, and you bleed.

Your anger has been a gift to me, your lioness's fierceness my saving
grace.
It has brought me out of myself, has taught me things I have struggled to
know.
It has called up my own anger, my own passion, my own whole self.

When you wash my feet I am overcome by my love for you.
When you lift me from the chair I am like a child in your arms.
I tell you now, my love, that my gratitude has no end.

What keeps me alive, what keeps me writing,
what keeps me whole and myself, is my trust and belief in Life itself,
a trust our whole history has prepared me for, trust your love has instilled
in me.

You gave me a confidence in the world I never had.
You gave me peace I truly never knew.
You gave me life, as you do now, every day.

We were married, we made our vows to each other,
we confirmed our love for each other before God and our people,
they joined with us in confirming and supporting our love for each other.

Your love for me, I know now, is stronger than death.
Your passion for life more fierce than the grave
Its flashes are flashes of fire, a raging flame

Many waters will never cool our love, nor floods drown
it I have set you as a seal upon my heart.
This is my love poem for you, oh my love.

Letter From Pluto

Just for the record –
I'm pissed at having to do something,
anything, for anyone else.
Don't ask me
to write a thank-you note,
to take out the trash, to get the oil changed;
don't expect me to respond to your phone call – I
won't. Yes, I'm the one in charge.
I've spent fifty years looking out
for everybody else first.
Argue with me if you will.
Tell me that I'm selfish.
Leave me alone if you choose.
I'll find out now who my friends are.
When you email me, you won't get a reply
unless it serves my own understanding
of my own ill-gotten hard-won
fifty years in the making freight train
disease. Don't get me wrong,
I appreciate your help, all your lovingkindness
over half a century, whoever you are,
but this now is my time. Don't fuck with me.
Don't fuck with me. Don't fuck
with me.
Because it's 3:30 in the morning and I can't sleep.
Because all you assholes are wanting this or that, well
I'm tired of keeping score,
I'm tired of counting up chits. I'm tired
of everything being a test of my allegiance
or productivity.
There's only one test now, and that is
does it help me live or die.
Living to me now
means keeping to myself: my oatmeal,
my one significant reader,
and, I suppose, the Devil Himself,
or God, whichever He is.

Fuck W.H. Auden and his Jamesian gymnastics,
his mirrors and petty squabbles with Shakespeare,
fuck him and his Ariel, his Caliban, grandiose
bigmouth that he is.
I don't have the time just now.
I gave at the office.
I'm on my own time.
Fuck you.

Going Deeper

I never felt at home there,
though we designed and even built some of it together,
never let myself sink down. I never relaxed.
Never let down a root. I never
felt at home there.
It's been seven years since I left,
and I can see, now, sometimes,
that it maybe had more of me in it
than I ever gave myself credit for.
Perhaps I did have something to do
with its tall windows that let in so much light,
its white plaster walls that Raven did for us.
She was a wizard with plaster, no doubt about that.
I did approve of all the choices.
I just didn't devise them. She did.
I learned so much from her over the years
that I am so grateful for, about what is beautiful,
what is pleasing to the eye, what is appropriate,
even sublime proportion, how to tell
a good color from it's ever so slightly different cousin
that's got just a little too much yellow.
But the house was hers, at least as far
as my fucked up psyche was concerned, and though
I loved being there, a part of me always felt like a guest.
In my own house. Just the way I feel in the house
I live in now.
                    So, whose fault was it? Hers?
That's what I told myself. She took up too much space,
her outsized presence always
in my face, always telling me what to do,
nothing I ever did was good enough.
O how I wish now I could have let that go –
no – fought her for my share of that space. I didn't know,
I never imagined, it was impossible to imagine
simply taking it. Taking my space.
She always said it herself.
Why couldn't I see how right she was?

Why couldn't I have taken her advice?
I had no fight in me, and she wasn't going
to just let that space go without a fight.
I dismissed it out of hand, thinking
that she was exactly wrong,
that she needed to lay down her weapons
and leave me in peace.
What then I thought was peace
is now cancer.

I have one memory, different from the rest,
from the construction phase.
When Spike McCullough dug the cellar hole
he couldn't quite get deep enough
because the ledge in one or two places
was a little too hard to break up with the bulldozer.
If we wanted to be able to stand in the basement
we'd have to break it out ourselves, he said,
to go a little deeper.
                            We rented a jackhammer
and one of those big air compressors
on its own wheels. We put on gloves,
and earplugs, goggles, and went at it. Everybody has seen them
in a construction zone at one time or another.
Everyone knows that incredible sound:
exploding air, steel breaking rock, thick dust, sweat.
You have seen and have imagined
the tremendous shaking of the upper body,
but you have never been inside that scene,
never been at the center of it, handles in your hands,
a mastery over more destruction than you'll ever have again,
the power to break up things that don't usually break,
quartz and granite, your whole body shaking,
the violence, the dust, the pounding steel point.

That memory somehow is not tainted
by shame like the rest of the memories,
of feeling like I was being dragged along
and hounded into helping with decisions

that would be hers in the end anyway –
so she could feel less alone, I guess.
I guess she must have felt alone. It didn't stop her.

Digging a hole. Breaking up rock. Going deeper.
These are the things I still need to be doing now
if I am going to continue to live in this life,
continue to wear the garment of this body.
At least that's what they tell me.
And I believe them, only
I don't know all the concrete steps to take.
I don't know what it is I'm supposed to do.
I don't know what the tools are.
I don't have the manual.

Food

O Christ.
Death this, death that.
I used to throw death's name around like he was a movie star
that I had brushed by in an airport once,
with his shades and fancy do and his earring and his entourage, such
     glitter, such glam.
We all die. Death is not so special.
The doctor says I have six months to live.
I don't believe him for a minute, that asshole,
but my guts are all suspended in a big sack of fluid
that makes up the middle of my self
for the last three days now.
And if I wasn't on friendly terms with food before
There certainly doesn't seem to be much room down there now for
     anything else.
Whenever I stand up I want to belch
and every time I belch it hurts, like there isn't room
for a gas bubble to float to the surface down there
through whatever tube it's got to travel
through all that weepy cancer fluid to get to the top.
Hiccups, too. I'm sure someone could tell me why hiccups
happen so much more often when you have
stomach difficulties due to cancer. I keep forgetting to ask.
Yes, I do take the morphine. I am more miserable without it,
believe me. Every tiny move I make and even
without moving at all these long muscles around my middle
have to stretch. They're sore. They're not used to having to do this.

There's a small rational voice underneath all the din of voices
from a hundred places around my body all complaining
about how tough they have it.
The small voice is clear, it says, hey,
this is a potentially dangerous situation here.
Yes, your weight is stable. But everyone says
you look skinnier. You know that in the mirror
the bones across your shoulders all stick out. You know
that there are several pounds of fluid in your gut

that don't really count toward your weight.
At least yesterday every couple of hours your stomach rumbled
telling you to go eat something. And yesterday
you were genuinely thirsty much of the day and drank a few glasses
of something, I don't know what.
Today food and drink do not call.
They stayed at home, feeling unwelcome.
You need to go out and find them again.
You don't want to have too many days like this one.
You need food. You need to figure this out.

A Cave In Late Winter

I took the day and stayed home.
I did not go to work.
I needed a day to myself, I said,
but what if one day is not enough?
What if one day becomes two, two
become four? What if the days lengthen,
all of them together a long afternoon
in late winter, when the sun advances
ever so slowly, and the light grows
day by day more golden
and dusky. The crows
will carouse at the compost pile.
The chickens grip their perch and wait,
the snow drip off the roof in steady rhythm.
The sun, the day, the hour, the life, advances.

I left the house. I put on my snowshoes.
I crossed the wooded hill on the contour,
counting the trees as I wove my way,
one two, three, four. On my left
the hill went rising to the crest, the slope
to the trace below on the right.
I came eventually to a ravine, and started to climb.
First one heavy snowshoe-laden foot,
and then another. Up, and over, I followed
the ravine down. Down, I followed it
for a long time. I heard the water
running underneath the snow below me,
I heard one squirrel cracking open a beech nut.
The rest was still, and white, until
I came to a cave. There was the smell
of woodsmoke, and some muddy footprints.
I took off my shoes.
I set them aside, and I went in.
There was the old man, as solid
and corporeal as ever, and I was tempted
to poke him with a finger and make him flinch.

He looked up once, then back at the ashes.
I was the first to speak. I said I thought
he was dead. He said no. He poked at his coals
with a stick that smoldered when he took
it out of the embers. He threatened me,
saying he would burn my eyes out.
He said he had never meant me any harm,
but there was nothing of him, not the
leathery folds in his face, not his crossed legs,
not his worn coat, not his wizened hands,
not the circles he made in the fire with his stick,
that called itself believable, or anything
but liar and cheat.

When I stood up, he leaned back, a little afraid.
I took his hand, and then dismantled him
bone by bone, separating each at the joint,
and I laid them all up in a neat pile.
Bleached they were, white
like the snow outside.
I laid the worn coat over them,
and the stick
I took with me
as I left.

What I Owe

In the middle of the night, at 4:00am,
the chickens, my three hens, at the far end of the garden
safe in their coop, rest oblivious on their sleep-smooth tree-branch perch,
and I am wandering around the house as if it were broad daylight
pecking and scratching, trying a bit of dry toast
here, half a banana there. The cancer is in the bone, but it's because
my bowels still aren't straight that I can't sleep, what I eat
turning over and back, from day to day alternately slipping
out like slip my brother dips his pots in, or locked up tight,
rock solid, immoveable, as if to say: try and make me.
                                                    The new diagnosis
is a week old, but I'm still in that state of wakefulness,
alert, of sharpened senses, a keen eye, a supple mind directed by a will
to get on with it: we did the research, located the doctor
in Denmark of all places, explored flights and prices,
and one stone at a time opened up those chinks
in that wall built up by whatever as yet hidden decisions,
debts real and imagined, that also, I suspect, resulted in the cancer itself:
I talked to my ex-wife
about helping out with the money; I threw caution to the wind
and tried to spell it out as best I could, what's happening,
what I'm going to do about it, to each boy, one at a time in that afternoon
space in the waning school year when that certain slant of light
has largely been replaced by bright green leaves and a high sun.

And every day a note home to the folks
to keep them up on what the doctors say,
to show them that I'm still here, walking, talking,
working it all out, and not afraid, too much anyway,
but still attacking it like a scientist, or student,
or something, anything, I guess it doesn't matter what, now
making a supreme effort not to guess
at what I think they want – or don't – to hear.
Presence, is all they want, I know, I owe them that,
at least. But nothing more.
Nothing more.

The Stick

When Jesus was a boy, he went around with a book.
He carried it through the marketplace until
he left. He was 12. He didn't sneak off. He followed his nose,
going where he had to go, no thought to whether his parents
would be worried or not. They were.
They panicked. But when they found him they had to be still.
Probably they were happy in their way. It's what parents want,
in the end: their children's freedom. Don't they?

When Jesus was a man, he went around with a stick.
Using it judiciously, he swung it
to and fro as he walked. He did a lot of walking,
town to town, village to village, up and down
the dusty dry roads of Palestine,
the stick swinging in time to his purposeful, measured,
unhurried gait. He was in this for the long haul.
God had other ideas.

In Jerusalem, Jesus had other uses for the stick.
He threatened demons. With varying degrees of insistence
he urged on the lame. The blind also, though they could only feel
the air flutter their eyelashes, the shadow of the sun
across their eyelids, and smell the mineral smell
of the clay dug with the big ash stick
to be mixed with Christ's own holy saliva
for that sight-giving potion.

The moneychangers in the Temple saw something else.
Raw anger, Jesus' own, brought up
from the very source of the earth, of life itself, from God –
called up through his gut, through his own glorious
ultimate openness to the source of Everything.
Coins scattered, men cursed,
table legs cracked with repeated sharp reports.
He was mad now, and they thought he was crazy.

***

When I was a small child, anger meant danger,
fearful, life-threatening, extinguishing, annihilating.
Out of my father it exploded,
or threatened to, every day.

I taught myself to be even smaller, to stay out of the way,
to shrink, to become invisible.
Naturally reticent, I knew how to keep quiet, and perfected it.
I learned not to speak. I kept close to my mother.

The booming voice was Sweeney's pike and Ronan's curse
and I was carried a long time, many years,
banished like Sweeney to the hills.
As a school boy, three pm marked the hour of anxiety,
my own time addled with anxiety until the dinner hour – this is what I
      remember.
The straightening of the papers on the coffee table,
arrangement just so of the cast off sneakers underneath.
Anything could set him off.

When I left home, the tables turned.
My parents switched roles – now father
found a listening ear. Mother
retreated, and never directing it at me,
keeping it hidden even from herself,
let her own rage seep and bleed
as if from a river Styx, deep down.

Beyond her own knowing
she turned it on anyone perceived
to have the power to separate us.
This is what I experienced.
This time anger itself stayed invisible,
acting on me unknown
As if from the river where the wrathful wreck
in the murky, muddy waters.

***

When I was a boy I went around with a book.
Climbed a tree in the back yard on the hill,
sat on a heavy limb overlooking the neighborhood
on a pillow my sister had sewn,
looked down occasionally to note the comings and goings
of squirrels and chipmunks in the brush
and the children in the street below,
A spy up on my perch, across the yard, up the hill:

There in my retreat I was an unwitting Sweeney
condemned by myself
to fearful, unending restlessness, anxious flitting
from tree to tree, thorn to thorn, hawthorn, buckthorn, blackthorn,
cursed by Ronan, fleeing friend and foe alike,
their stiff arrows, their pointed spears,
avoiding at all cost a confrontation
the chance of being pinned to a stump,

gutted like a chicken,
ill fortune told in my own entrails
scattered across a bench.
Day by day. Year by year. From infancy
to diapers, to grade school and on
into adolescence and never quite out
I carried my books, or nothing, and went barehanded
and weaponless through the days and years

of extended traveling post-adolescent unwitting
hiding in trees. Tangled in Sweeney's
ever present thorns, cut and bloody
and skinned over again and again
while anger grew in the gut. There from the beginning,
before birth, before proto-seed,
before the chicken, before the egg.
Before inhabiting a body I brought it here with me

from wherever I came, packed carefully

in my newborn's suitcase,
my fat bag of tricks, my articles of faith, my tools of the trade
to be used as best I could in the business
of being a human being on Earth, beginning
on that day they ask me to repeat
every time they check my bracelet
in the infusion room: "Four-seven-sixty-one."

***

I am not an old man.
But now I carry another stick, aluminum,
for which I find myriad uses.
I can put an old man's plastic diaper on without squatting,
snaking my feet through the holes
opened with the butt end.
I can open and shut the bathroom door, flick
two lights on, lift the lid,

hang the cane on the shower curtain bar
and get the pee in the john without spilling.
Unable to bend over, I can jimmy the bottom bathroom drawer
to look for a nail clipper.
I can use the hook end
if I've left my book, notebook, paper, pencils
out of reach, pulling them across my lap
making a show of doing something.

The cancer grew out of the anger as I, witless,
always in a hurry to avoid the work of being human,
of using emotion for the building of something,
letting it move through me, reaching, as emotion does,
toward heaven. Anger connects us from the gut
to the stars, I see that now. Every time I felt it rising up hot
I left it lidded there. Instead I lit a small candle for anger
and encouraged it to rest in peace.

After many years it finally knocked me down
and landed me in the hospital.

It swelled my body like a balloon,
reduced my day's work to the basic bodily functions,
and yet proved a blessing to have to think of nothing else,
to let someone do for me after all these years
I was convinced I had to perform, had to produce,
had to give and not receive in order to be justified.

When I couldn't walk without that cane,
get up and down stairs,
in or out of the car
or get up out of a chair,
when I couldn't get into bed myself,
make my own meal, or do for myself
in almost any way you can imagine,
I finally let go.

I finally let go, because of the one
without whom, I tell you now,
I would not exist. Angel of mercy,
my beloved, my fair one,
for whom love is as strong as death, passion
as fierce as the grave. She who has brought me,
finally, after all these years peace, trust,
confidence in God's world I never had.

She washed my swollen legs and feet,
she ministered to my open sores,
arranged my body in bed so I could sleep at night,
cooked, cleaned, laundered,
ran an entire complicated household
and still she responded to the demands
of her own children, and took on even more
of the parenting of mine.

I slept. I let go of every responsibility
And she took each one up. I only let myself worry
about "getting well," which was no worry,
asleep as I was to how sick I really was.
No phone calls, no mail, nothing.

Anger slept. All emotion slept
while I got through my days
one swollen footstep at a time.

I thought I was finished with anger.
But as she nursed me back, anger came back.
Sometimes I dreamed at night
of swinging that cane, of clearing the decks
of all my pill bottles in the bathroom,
of shouting and breaking things.
Because I'm angry. I want out,
out of this disease, out of the work it takes

every day to piss and shit, and out, too,
of this feeling sorry for myself.
It isn't fair. It shouldn't be me,
let someone else be the butt
of God's cruel joke.
Still, I'm not done yet.
I'm on the chemo now. There's strength returning
for another round with God.

Last week we went to church,
and the place that used to feel welcoming
felt alien and distant. I thought,
even Jesus knew nothing about death
until right at the end.
But I know it was the stick
that kept him from cancer.
I long to take his lead

and wield his stick
and swing my cane
until all the crashing has happened,
the shards of all my fragile fortress
come crumbling down uncountable,
the landscape of all
my fearful family relations
laid flat and waste,

every rough place plane
in preparation for my coming, finally,
with some luck,
and will, and a stout stick
to some semblance of satisfaction
with the sorry suitcase full of work
I brought with me when I first came
this time over the threshold.

Stage 4 Hormone Resistant

Near death
though unaware
before the chemo worked,
awareness holds my hand and won't
let go.

New Years Day 1/1/11
East Side, Providence, Rhode Island

Woke up late. Read later. Michael J. Bradley.
Swallowed a hard boiled egg.
Ran to yoga. Made me
want to throw up.
Ate oatmeal and scrambled eggs.
Still wanted to pass out.
Walked to Indian Point Park
with A and her mom, B.
Salt water, slush,
man jumping rope on the jetty.
Packed kids in car. JCC
was closed. Played bball
at the outside courts till
after dark. Helped make
and eat pizza. With stones,
and windows open
for fear of CO.
Kitchen still
the warmest place
in the house.

Prayer

Who am I
to compare myself to Job? I'm forty-eight,
and since the year that I turned forty-five
I've only lost job, home, career, marriage,
health, lover, and life savings,
and no prospects yet, no dim outline
of the way in which any of those things
might return. Dear God, in all seriousness, don't
let me be separated, by death
or loneliness, or any of your
dramatic accidents – the house collapsing
in a violent storm, a dread disease,
the body feeding on itself in boils,
a freak head-on across the median,
or misjudged icing on the curve
above the river, guardrail giving way,
or my own God-damned self-absorption –
from my children.
                        You know how poor Job
had to keep losing, loss upon brutal, heart-breaking loss
until he would speak up.

Fishing
Shag Harbour, Nova Scotia

We tried every day:
mackerel hooks, flies,
the famous "spinnow,"
risked our lives pulling
periwinkles from
the pilings for bait
("wrinkles" they called them),
waited for high tide,
tried morning, noon, night,
off wharves, the causeway
and a borrowed boat
smelling of fish. Each
day we started out
with one more story
from a lobsterman,
off-season, with time
on his hands, telling
about what rig, what
bait, no bait, where, when –
and ended up with
still nothing.
     And then,
next day, nonplussed, not
hopeful, tried again.

Christmas Gift

Here he was almost nine years old
at Christmas when the kitten turned up
in a box with holes and a bow under the tree.
His little brother knew right away
what it was, tore off the wrapping
and scooped it up, hugging it to his chest,
a fuzzy thing with a quizzical look,
limp and dangling from his arms.
Sammy seemed as delighted as any of us
but we noticed as the morning progressed
that he admired it from a safe distance
and moved away whenever it got too close.
"Pick it up," we all said, and he replied,
confident as a saint, "I don't touch live animals."
As if it were a fact as plain as snow.
After a day or two
I got him to tell me what it was, something
about the way a kitten feels
inside its loose bag of skin, the bones
and organs sliding around under your fingers,
too fragile, I think, too close
to the huge, impossible, fearful mystery
of what makes a bag of guts animate,
and lovely, and alive, and able somehow
to love us in return.

Eight A.M.

The fog
obscures the view
of everything except
your kitchen table, notebook, and
yourself.

Jay Rossier

Jay Rossier (1961-2012), author of "Living With Chickens" (Lyons Press, 2002), was a skilled man and had multiple careers throughout his life. A freelance writer for "Chickens" magazine, Jay was the local guy people sought out with questions in regard to their birds. He had a passion for animals. As a young man, following in the footsteps of his native Vermont ancestors, he enjoyed working on a dairy farm in the Midwest.

A soap-maker, a Waldorf teacher, a singer in the Thetford Chamber Singers, an editor, a computer consultant, an artist, a traveler, a mathematician, a baker, Jay was a true Renaissance man, a kind and gentle soul with a perpetual twinkle in his eye, a seeker of all that is subtle and interesting and beautiful in life.

Made in the USA
Middletown, DE
15 July 2018